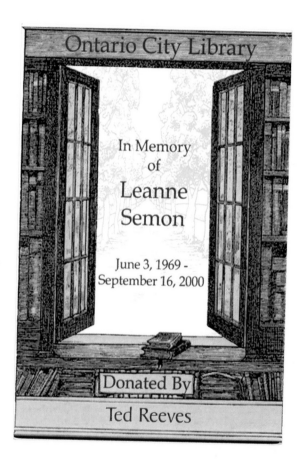

Thinking and Feeling

Angela Royston

RIGBY
INTERACTIVE
LIBRARY

© 1997 Rigby Education
Published by Rigby Interactive Library,
an imprint of Rigby Education,
division of Reed Elsevier, Inc.
500 Coventry Lane
Crystal Lake, IL 60014

Interiors designed by Inklines and Small House Design
Illustrations by Gary Rees, p. 4, p. 9, p. 20 (right), p. 22; John Bovosier, p. 8;
Peter Bull Art Studiop: p. 12, p. 14, p. 16, p. 20 (left), p. 24, p. 27; Frank Kennard, p. 10.

Printed in the United Kingdom

00 99 98 97 96
10 9 8 7 6 5 4 3 2 1

Library of Congress Cataloging-in-Publication Data

Royston, Angela.
   Thinking and feeling / Angela Royston.
      p. cm. – (Body systems)
Includes bibliographical references and index.
Summary: Describes the parts of the human body that enable us to perceive the world,
think, and move our muscles.
   ISBN 1-57572-095-7 (library)
      1. Nervous system – Juvenile literature. 2. Thought and thinking – Juvenile literature.
3. Senses and sensation – Juvenile literature. [1. Nervous system. 2. Senses and sensation.
3. Thought and thinking. 4. Brain]
I. Title. II. Series: Body systems (Crystal Lake, Ill.)
QP361.5.R69 1997
612.8 – dc20

                                                        96-29403
                                                           CIP
                                                           AC

Acknowledgments

The publisher would like to thank the following for permission to reproduce photographs:
Barnaby's Picture Library, p. 4; Corbis/Bettmann, p. 7 (bottom); Image Bank, p. 13;
"PA" Photo Library (Press Association/Topham), p. 5; Sally and Richard Greenhill, p. 15 (bottom);
Science Photo Library, p. 9, p. 15 (top), p. 21, p. 27, p. 28, p. 29; Telegraph Color Library, p. 25;
Tony Stone Images, p. 6, p. 7 (top), p. 11 (both), p. 17 (both), p. 18, p. 23, p. 26.
Commissioned photograph p. 19: Trevor Clifford.

Every effort has been made to contact copyright holders of any material reproduced in this book.
Any omissions will be rectified in subsequent printings if notice is given to the publisher.

> **Note to the Reader**
> Some words in this book are printed in **bold** type. This indicates that the word is listed in the
> glossary on pages 30–31. This glossary gives a brief explanation of words that may be new to you.

Visit Rigby's Education Station® on the World Wide Web at http://www.rigby.com

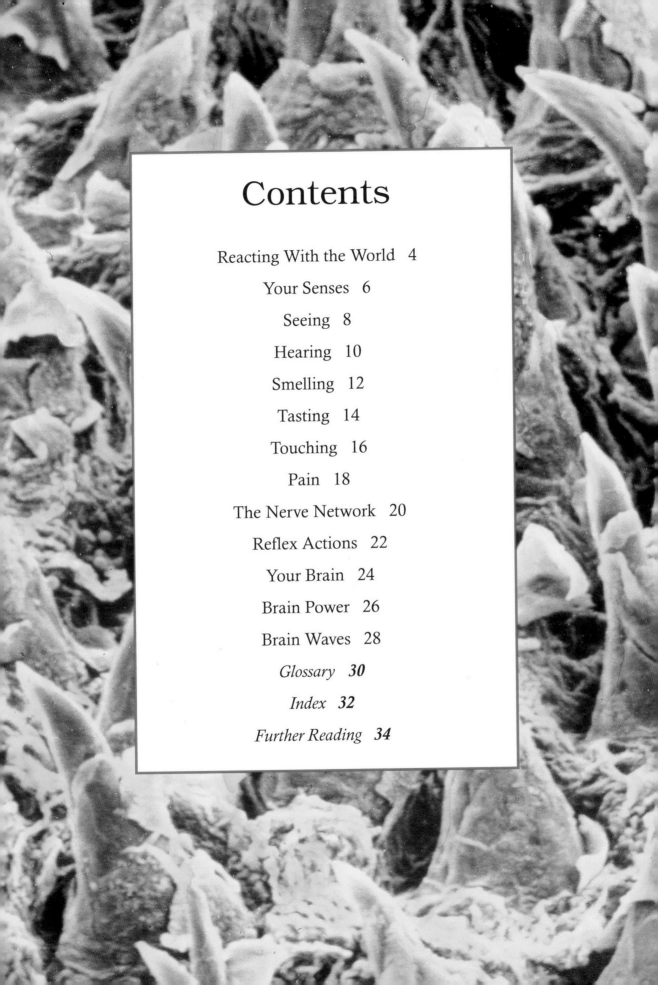

Contents

Reacting With the World 4

Your Senses 6

Seeing 8

Hearing 10

Smelling 12

Tasting 14

Touching 16

Pain 18

The Nerve Network 20

Reflex Actions 22

Your Brain 24

Brain Power 26

Brain Waves 28

Glossary 30

Index 32

Further Reading 34

Reacting to the World

What if suddenly you could not see, hear, taste, smell, or feel a touch? What would you know of the world around you? Nothing. Your eyes, ears, nose, tongue, and skin are your **sense organs.** They pick up impressions from the world and send messages about them to your **brain.** Your brain sorts the messages and interprets them, or decides what they mean. Then your brain sends messages to your **muscles,** telling them how to respond. All these messages are carried by your **nerves.**

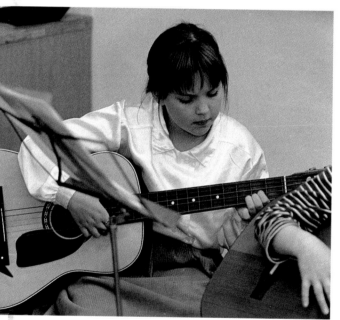

Your nervous system

Your sense organs, nerves, and brain form a communication system in your body, called the **nervous system.** Nerves are like fine electrical wires that carry signals from the **senses** to the brain and from the brain to the muscles. The brain itself is a soft ball made up of millions of **nerve cells,** connected together in countless different ways.

▲ This girl is using her senses to play the guitar. She feels the strings with her fingers and hears their sound with her ears. Her brain interprets the sounds and tells her fingers what to do.

► Nerves carry messages to the brain from the senses and from the brain to the muscles telling them to act.

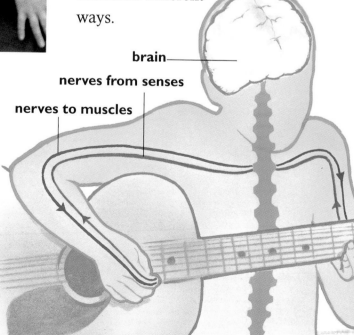

brain—

nerves from senses

nerves to muscles

4

◄ You use your brain for everything you do and feel. When you are watching a football game, your brain interprets signals from your eyes to tell you what is happening and it makes you feel excited, pleased, or disappointed at what you see.

Your brain

Your brain is responsible for everything you think, feel, and know. Even many high-powered computers working together could not do what your brain does. You can plan ahead, decide whether something is good or bad, and experience many different emotions, including happiness, anger, and excitement with your brain. Your brain continuously receives information from your sense organs and sends messages to the muscles.

You are not aware of everything that your brain does. It controls all the other systems in your body. For example, it triggers the muscles that you use to breathe air in and out of your **lungs,** so that even when you are fast asleep, you continue to breathe. It controls every aspect of your **digestive system**—including the muscles that push food through the intestines and the glands that make digestive juices. It also controls your liver, kidneys, and other internal organs.

Did you know?

Your body is made up of billions of tiny cells. Muscles, bones, blood, skin, nerves, and so on, are each built of a different kind of cell. Nerve cells are different shapes and sizes. The nerve cells in the brain are the smallest kind of cell in the body— only 1/25,000 of an inch thick!

The Senses

How do we discover the world around us? Even as newborn babies, we begin to explore the things near to us through our **senses.** A baby soon recognizes its mother's face or father's voice. Sight and hearing are just two of your five senses. The other three are smell, taste, and touch. Between them, these senses tell you everything you know about the world. They gather information that your brain then sorts out and uses.

Gathering information

Your eyes, ears, nose, tongue and skin are sense organs. They have special **receptors** that detect a particular **stimulus.** Receptors in your eyes detect light. Those in your ears detect sound waves. Tiny particles of chemicals **stimulate** smell and taste. Receptors in your skin and deep inside your body pick up heat, cold, pressure, and pain. When they are stimulated, they send **electrical signals** along your nerves to your brain.

Bombarded with information

Your senses bombard your brain with information all the time. Your brain quickly interprets the signals and ignores the unimportant ones. Although you can hear the traffic outside, you probably don't notice it until a fire engine races by. You can feel the pages of this book, but you may not notice that you do. Often, you notice things touching your body only if they make you uncomfortable.

▶ *The girls eating these pieces of orange can see, smell, and taste them. They can also feel the orange in their hands and the sticky juice on their lips.*

Coordination

What you sense and what you do work together. Your brain becomes so quick at coordinating the two that you do many things without thinking. Your eyes tell you where some object is, your hand moves to it, and you pick it up. You may have trouble coordinating your movements and senses when you first try something new, such as a video game. You have to learn how the keys affect the screen. But after a while the links between sight, sound, and touch become automatic, and you play the game without thinking about the keys.

▼ To play a computer game, you have to learn to quickly coordinate what your fingers do with what your eyes see on the screen.

◄ Helen Keller became blind and deaf before she had learned to speak, so she could not imitate the sounds of speech. Instead she put her hand over her teacher's lips and throat and learned to copy the movement and vibrations she felt.

Did you know?
Helen Keller could not talk or communicate with anyone until a teacher named Annie Sullivan taught her to communicate using only the sense of touch. Annie slowly and patiently taught Helen to read Braille and even to speak.

Seeing

Your eye works like a camera. The black circle in the center of your eye is a hole called the pupil. It is covered by a transparent window called the **cornea.** Light enters your eye through the cornea and the pupil. It then passes through the lens which focuses it so that a clear but upside-down "picture" forms on the **retina** at the back of your eye. **Nerve endings** in the retina send the picture to your brain.

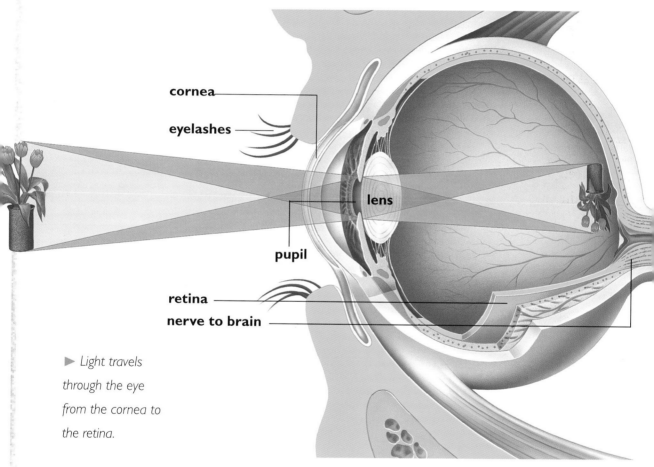

cornea
eyelashes
lens
pupil
retina
nerve to brain

▶ Light travels through the eye from the cornea to the retina.

Color or black and white?

The back of the retina is lined with two kinds of light-sensitive cells called rods and cones. Cones detect different colors but work well only in bright light. Rods work best in dim light but don't detect color.

That is why everything looks gray or black in dim light. When light falls on rods and cones, it triggers electrical signals. These pass from the nerve endings along the nerve fibers to the **optic nerve.** The optic nerve carries the signals to the brain.

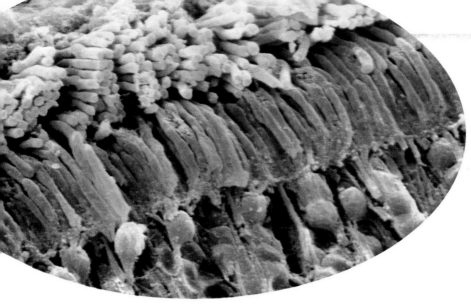

Learning to see

Although we say that a picture is formed on the retina, it is not a picture like a photograph. What the brain receives is a changing pattern of electrical signals, like those that make a picture on your television screen. The brain interprets the signals to make the picture that you see.

Babies must learn to "see." They first recognize simple patterns, then slowly learn to distinguish more complicated shapes and colours. Blind people who regain their sight also have to learn to make sense of the world around them.

▲ If you look at this drawing one way, it looks like two faces. If you look at it another way, it looks like a vase. Your brain can make sense of this picture in two different ways.

Did you know?

The retina makes color pictures rather like a TV screen does. Some cones react only to red light, others only to blue, and others only to green. Every other color is a combination of these three. Some people are 'color blind'. Either their cones do not work properly or there is something wrong with the nerve to the brain. Either way, they cannot tell all the colors apart, particularly red and green. More boys than girls suffer from some color blindness—about 8 males in every 100.

Hearing

If you bang a drum you can hear a sound. You might also feel the drum quivering, or vibrating. The air around it vibrates, too. These vibrations are sound waves. You can't see these waves, but they spread out like ripples on a pond. Some of the sound waves reach your ears and pass down the ear canal to the eardrum. The vibrations then travel through your ear to the nerves that send signals to your brain.

Journey through the ear

The **outer ear** is the part you can see. It is a flap of skin and **cartilage** that picks up sound waves. These make your eardrum vibrate. The eardrum divides the outer ear from the three bones of the **middle ear.** These small, delicate bones pick up vibrations from the eardrum and magnify them. From the middle ear, sound waves pass through the oval window into the inner ear. Inside is the **cochlea,** a spiral tube that looks like a snail's shell. The cochlea is filled with liquid. Nerve cells in the cohlea react to vibrations in the liquid, sending electrical signals along the **auditory nerve** to the brain. Your brain interprets the signals as sound.

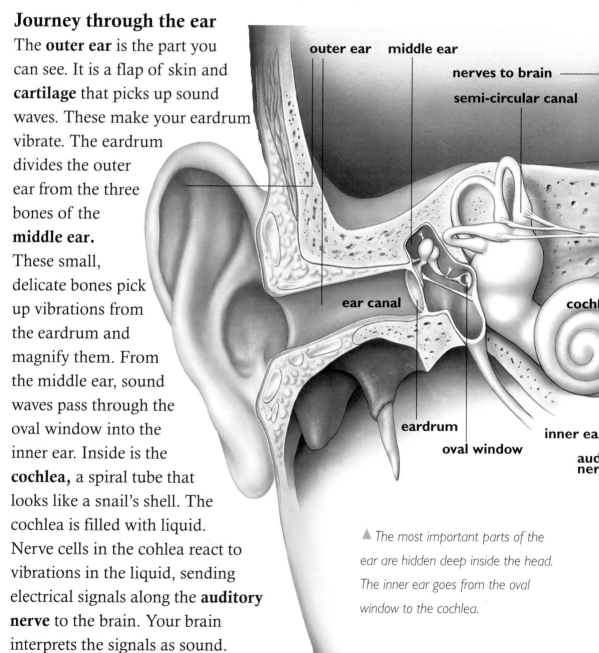

outer ear   middle ear

nerves to brain

semi-circular canal

ear canal

coch

eardrum

inner ea

oval window

aud
ner

▲ The most important parts of the ear are hidden deep inside the head. The inner ear goes from the oval window to the cochlea.

Balancing act

The inner ear also contains three semicircular canals filled with liquid. These three tubes are at right angles to each other and they help your sense of balance. Every time you move, the liquid in the semicircular canals moves too. Nerve endings in the canals send messages to the brain. You know what position your body is in because your brain knows how the liquid in the semicircular canals is moving.

▲ *Your sense of balance tells you which way up you are. The liquid inside this boy's semicircular canals tells him that he is upside-down.*

▶ *Loud noises can damage the delicate workings of the ear. This worker is wearing earmuffs to protect his ears from the noise of the drill.*

Did you know?

The loudness of sound is measured in decibels. A whisper is only about 30 decibels, and a loud alarm clock is about 80. Jackhammers can reach 100 decibels, but jet planes can reach an ear-splitting 140 decibels. Noises over 90 decibels can damage your hearing, and those over 165 decibels can even kill you.

Smelling

S ight and hearing are the senses you rely on the most, but smell is very important, too. When you smell something bad, such as rotting food, you know it may be harmful. What you smell are gases in the air, tiny floating **particles** that you breathe into your nose. When you sniff something to smell it better, you are trying to take more particles to your smell-detecting **cells.**

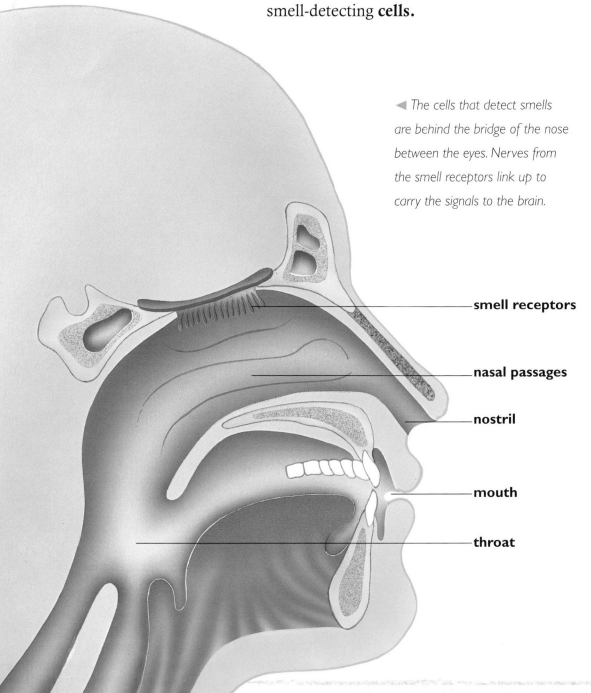

◀ *The cells that detect smells are behind the bridge of the nose between the eyes. Nerves from the smell receptors link up to carry the signals to the brain.*

smell receptors

nasal passages

nostril

mouth

throat

Inside the nose

Your nose is bigger than you may think. It stretches back into your head above your mouth. The two nostrils lead to **nasal passages** made by three pieces of bone. The nostrils and nasal passages are lined with **mucus** and tiny hairs that are there to catch dirt and germs. Smell receptors are sunk in a layer of mucus and respond only to particles that have dissolved in it.

Too much mucus, however, dulls the sense of smell. If you have a cold and your nose is blocked, no particles can get through the mucus to the smell receptors, and so you cannot smell anything. The sense of taste relies heavily on the sense of smell. Much of what you think is taste is really smell, so, if you can't smell, you cannot taste much either.

Smell and memory

Smells are often very closely linked with memory. The smell of suntan oil, for example, may make you think of last summer's vacation. The part of the brain that deals with smell is very close to the part that deals with memory. In fact, messages about smell pass through the memory area of the brain on their way to the smell area.

◀ Bad smells like those from rotting garbage warn us of possible danger.

Did you know?

There are about 5 million smell receptors at the top of each nostril. No one knows exactly how the brain tells one smell from another, but human beings can detect over 3,000 different smells. Many animals can do much better. A dog's sense of smell is over a million times more sensitive than ours. Dogs can track people from the smell of their footprints!

Tasting

Some people, such as chefs, can recognize many different tastes in just one mouthful of food. But most people do not have a very good sense of taste. They cannot even tell an apple from a pear if they shut their eyes and block their nose. The cells that detect taste are in the mouth, mainly on the tongue. The tip and edges of the tongue are covered with taste buds, which react to one of four basic tastes—salty, sweet, sour, and bitter. Every taste is either one or a combination of these.

▼ *Different parts of the tongue detect mainly one kind of taste.*

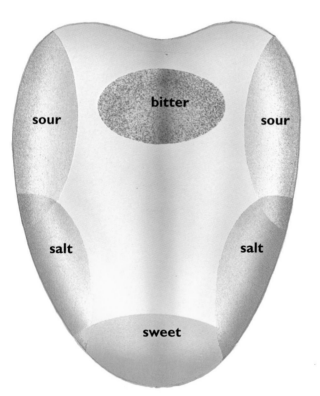

Your tongue

The surface of your tongue is rough and moist. The roughness comes from tiny **papillae**. Taste-buds in the papillae detect chemicals dissolved in saliva. Saliva, with food dissolved in it, flows through the opening of the taste-bud and stimulates the taste cells inside. When the taste cell is triggered, an electrical signal passes down the nerves to your brain. Somehow your brain puts together the signals from all the taste cells and produces the sense of taste.

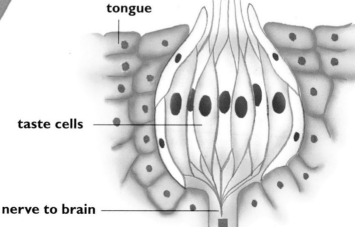

▶ *This taste bud has been enlarged thousands of times.*

◄ The surface of the tongue magnified over 335 times. This shows what a rough surface your tongue has.

Enjoying food

Your sense of taste alone is not very strong. It is helped by all the other senses. Think of a food you really like, cookies perhaps. The sight and smell of one makes your mouth water. As you bite into it, the smell increases. The sound of the crunching and the feel of the cookies in your mouth all add to the pleasure of eating. We human beings like the taste of sweet things from the moment we are born, but we don't usually like the taste of very bitter things.

▲ Medicine is good for you, but it often tastes bitter. Some medicines are sweetened to make them taste more pleasant.

Did you know?

If you look in the mirror and stick out your tongue, you will see a V-shaped row of papillae at the back of the tongue. These not only detect bitter tastes, they also help to protect you from poisons. If a taste is very bitter they trigger the "gag" reflex. You automatically spit out the bitter substance. You can't rely on the gag reflex, however: some poisons taste sweet.

Touching

Unlike the other senses, the receptors that respond to touch are found throughout your body, mainly in your skin. There are several kinds of touch receptors. Some nerve cells in the skin react to heat, some to cold, and others to touch, pressure, and pain.

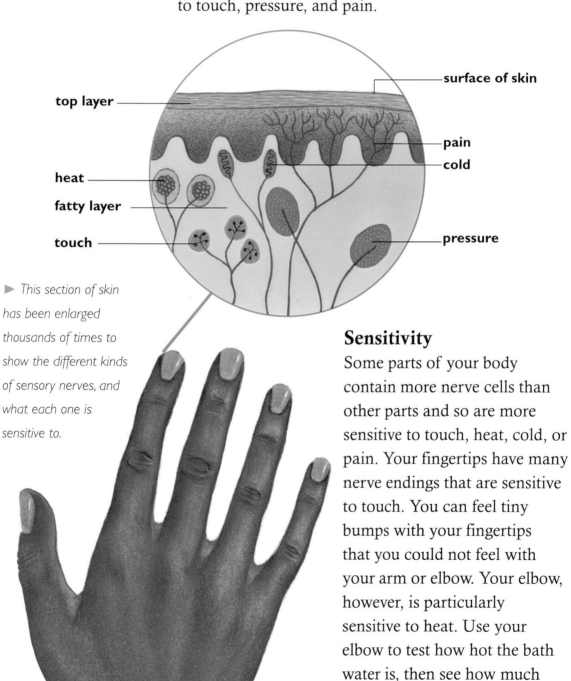

surface of skin

top layer

pain

cold

heat

fatty layer

touch

pressure

▶ *This section of skin has been enlarged thousands of times to show the different kinds of sensory nerves, and what each one is sensitive to.*

Sensitivity

Some parts of your body contain more nerve cells than other parts and so are more sensitive to touch, heat, cold, or pain. Your fingertips have many nerve endings that are sensitive to touch. You can feel tiny bumps with your fingertips that you could not feel with your arm or elbow. Your elbow, however, is particularly sensitive to heat. Use your elbow to test how hot the bath water is, then see how much cooler it feels to your hand.

◄ The sense of touch is important to all of us. Simply stroking a pet makes us feel more relaxed and happy.

▼ When you touch something, you may feel more than one sensation. For example, these icicles feel cold, smooth, and heavy.

Your lips and tongue are sensitive to touch, heat and cold. You test food with your lips to make sure it won't burn your mouth. And have you noticed that when a tooth falls out, the gap it leaves feels enormous to your tongue? Your back, however, has far fewer touch receptors. If someone touches you lightly on the back, you may not even feel it.

"Seeing" by feeling

Blind people tend to develop their sense of touch and use it instead of sight to find their way around. They use their fingers to feel objects around them and a stick to "feel" the pavement in front of them. **Braille** is a special alphabet of raised dots that blind people can read with their fingertips by touching the dots.

Did you know?

The very top layer of skin is dead. It consists of hard, tough cells that protect the living cells below. New skin cells are made in the lower layers and are slowly pushed up towards the surface. Old, dead cells rub off against your clothes and when you wash. In fact much of the dust in your house is made up of dead skin cells!

Pain

There are many more pain receptors than other kinds of nerve endings in your skin. So it is easier to say exactly where a pain is than where a feeling of pressure is. Pain is useful in telling you when something is wrong, but some people seem to feel pain more strongly than others. There are several kinds of pain. Pain receptors near the surface of the skin make you feel tickly or itchy. Those lower down give you stabbing pain. If even deeper pain receptors are triggered, you feel a dull, throbbing ache.

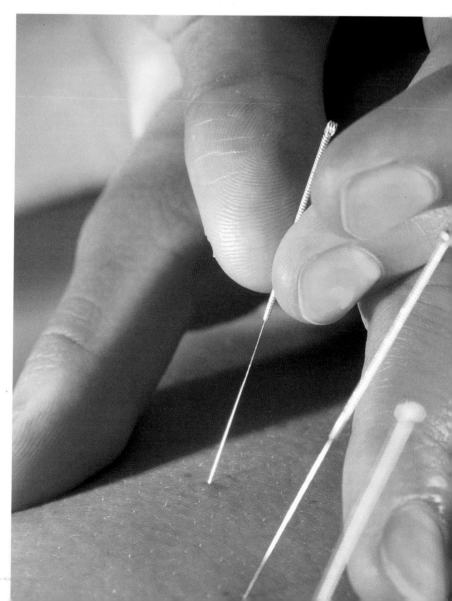

▶ *Some doctors use* **acupuncture** *instead of an anesthetic to stop their patients from feeling pain during an operation. The patient can stay awake throughout the operation without feeling any pain. Acupuncturists are specially trained so they know exactly where to place the needles.*

◀ *Unexpected pain makes you cry out in shock. It also makes you more careful next time!*

A useful warning

If you fall and hurt yourself, you usually feel pain. Pain stops you walking or running on a damaged ankle or leg, so the injury has time to heal. But the amount of pain does not necessarily show how bad the damage is. The prick of a thorn can be agonizing, while a deep cut may hardly hurt at all. Lepers know how important it is to be able to feel pain. Leprosy is a disease that can damage the nerve endings so that the person does not feel pain. Lepers are often scarred and injured because they don't notice when something is burning or injuring them.

Deadening pain

Anesthetics deaden or lessen pain. Some act on a part of the body (local anesthetic), some on the whole body (general anesthetic). A local anesthetic acts on particular nerve endings and connections. Football players and other athletes sometimes use local anesthetics to numb pain during a game so that they can go on playing. A general anesthetic makes a patient unconscious during an operation so that he or she feels no pain and is not aware of the operation.

Did you know?

Some people train themselves not to feel pain: they overcome the feeling of pain in the mind. Yogis in India lie on beds of nails and walk through fire. You can help yourself control pain without doing anything so dangerous. Fear can make pain feel worse. The next time you have an injection, try to relax and not pull away from the pain. If you can do this, it should be less painful.

The Nerve Network

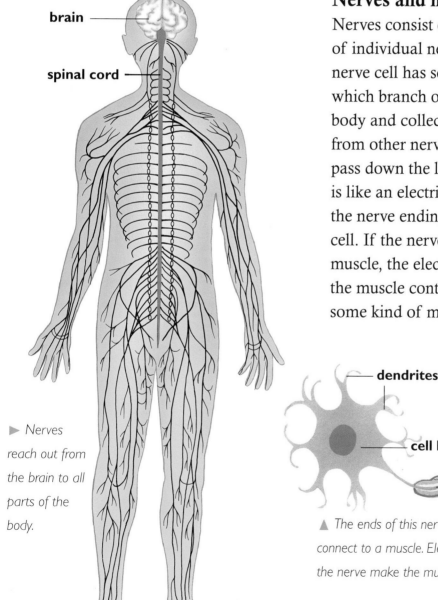

brain

spinal cord

► Nerves
reach out from
the brain to all
parts of the
body.

Nerves and nerve cells

Nerves consist of bundles of millions of individual nerve cells. Each motor nerve cell has several **dendrites,** which branch out around the cell body and collect electrical signals from other nerves nearby. The signals pass down the long, thin **axon,** which is like an electrical wire, and through the nerve endings to the next nerve cell. If the nerve endings join to a muscle, the electrical signals make the muscle contract which causes some kind of movement.

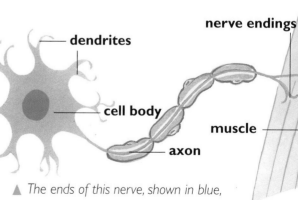

nerve endings

dendrites

cell body

axon

muscle

▲ The ends of this nerve, shown in blue, connect to a muscle. Electrical signals from the nerve make the muscle contract, or flex.

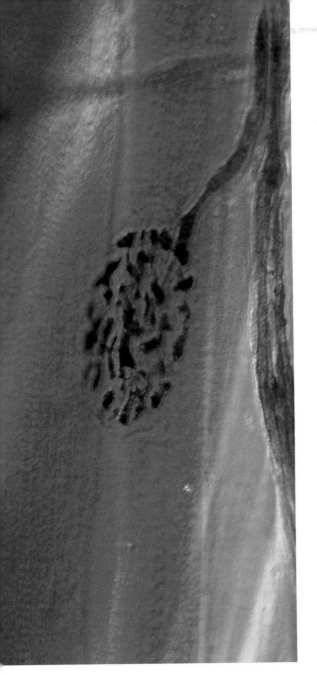

The spinal cord

The main highway for nerves to your body is the spinal cord. It is protected by a column of bones—the vertebrae that make up your spine. Pairs of nerves leave the spinal cord and split into smaller and smaller branches until they reach all over your body. Twelve pairs of nerves, however, do not go through the spinal cord. They connect your brain directly to your eyes, ears, mouth, nose, neck, and certain vital organs, such as your heart.

Paralysis

If the spinal cord is injured, some parts of the body may become paralyzed. The sensory nerves' messages can no longer get through and link with the muscles. How much of the body is paralyzed depends on how far up the spine the injury is. If the bottom of the spine is hurt, only the legs are affected. An injury to the neck, however, may paralyze most of the body.

▲ A single motor nerve cell magnified hundreds of times. It conducts electrical signals from the brain to the muscle.

Did you know?

Bare electrical wires are usually insulated with a plastic covering because they are very dangerous to touch. Similarly some nerve axons have an insulating covering. Usually, it is only the end of the nerve that needs to be sensitive—the rest of the nerve simply carries the message from the nerve endings to the brain.

Reflex Actions

Have you ever noticed that if you prick your finger, you pull it away even before you've noticed the pain? This is called a **reflex action.** The body acts fast, without waiting for the brain to realize what is happening. The nervous system can respond so quickly because some signals from the sensory nerves are relayed directly to the motor nerves in the spinal cord bypassing the brain. The motor nerves go into action while the rest of the signals travel on to the brain.

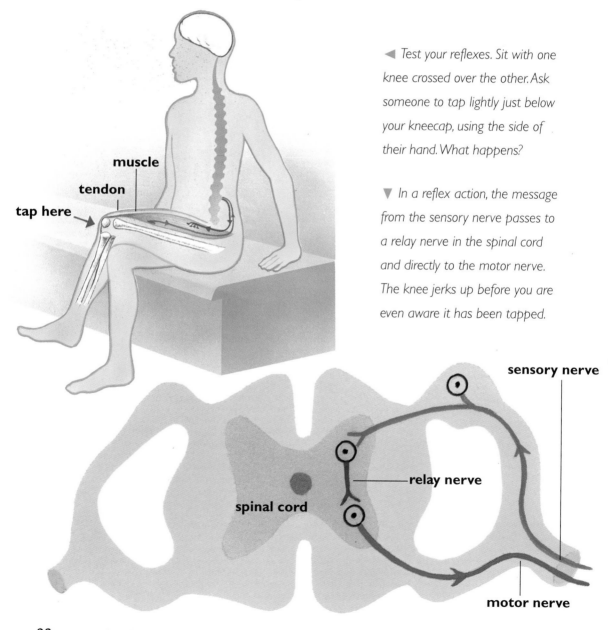

◀ *Test your reflexes. Sit with one knee crossed over the other. Ask someone to tap lightly just below your kneecap, using the side of their hand. What happens?*

▼ *In a reflex action, the message from the sensory nerve passes to a relay nerve in the spinal cord and directly to the motor nerve. The knee jerks up before you are even aware it has been tapped.*

muscle

tendon

tap here

sensory nerve

relay nerve

spinal cord

motor nerve

Knee-jerk reactions

Sit with one leg crossed over the other and ask someone to tap your leg lightly just below the kneecap. When they tap the right spot, your knee will jerk upward of its own accord. This is just one of many reflex actions you are born with. Blinking if something comes close to your eyes is also a reflex action. So is sneezing. If something tickles the inside of your nose it can be very hard to avoid sneezing. Swallowing is another reflex action. When a mouthful of food reaches the back of your throat, you automatically swallow it.

Working unawares

Some reflexes work without you even being aware of them. They are controlled by a special part of the brain and are called the **autonomic nervous system.** When you move from dim light to bright light, the pupil of your eye gets smaller to stop too much light entering the eye. When you are hot, the tiny blood vessels near the surface of your skin stretch so that more blood is brought to the surface to be cooled. Other parts of your body, such as your heart, digestive system, and kidneys, also work without you being aware of them.

► As these athletes get hot, their autonomic nervous system cuts in to help keep them cool.

Did you know?

Electrical signals travel much more slowly along the nerves than along electric wiring. Copper wiring carries electrical signals almost as fast as the speed of light (180,000 miles per second). The fastest nerve messages, such as those that make you blink, travel at only 394 feet per second, but they don't have far to go, so we don't usually notice any delay. The slowest signals, such as those that carry pain messages from your toes to your brain, may travel at only 3.3 feet per second.

Your Brain

If you could see your brain, it would look like a huge soft, gray wrinkled walnut. It is in fact a complex network of nerve cells supplied with blood. The blood feeds the nerve cells. Your whole brain is encased in a watery cushion which helps to protect it from bumps and bangs. Outside this is a thick covering of bone, the **skull**. The brain is divided into different parts, each with its own job to do.

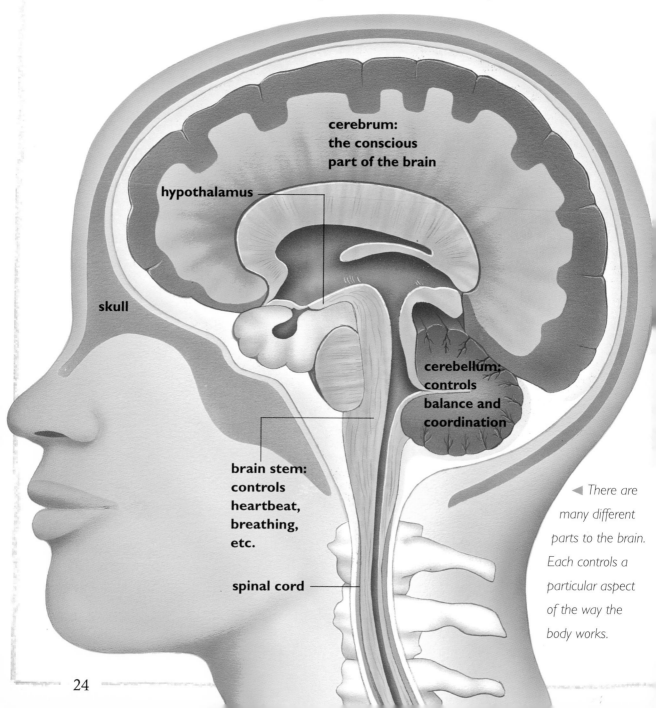

cerebrum: the conscious part of the brain

hypothalamus

skull

cerebellum: controls balance and coordination

brain stem: controls heartbeat, breathing, etc.

spinal cord

◄ There are many different parts to the brain. Each controls a particular aspect of the way the body works.

Cerebrum and cerebellum

The largest part of your brain is the **cerebrum.** This wrinkled mass makes up four-fifths of the whole and it controls everything you are aware of, such as thinking, remembering, and moving. It also processes information from your senses. The rest of the brain is hidden beneath the cerebrum. The **cerebellum** controls balance and coordinates messages to the motor nerves so that all your movements are smooth and controlled.

Brain stem

The **brain stem** controls the body systems that keep you alive, such as your breathing, digestion, and heartbeat. Special nerves, which form the autonomic nervous system, leave the brain stem and go directly to your heart and to the muscles that control digestion and breathing. These messages do not normally reach the cerebrum, so you are not aware of them.

At the top of the brain stem is the **hypothalamus**. It controls the temperature of your body and links to feelings such as thirst, hunger, anger, and pleasure. Strangely, the nerves cross over in the brain stem, so that the left side of your brain controls the right side of your body, and the right side of the brain controls the left side of your body.

◄ *These athletes are sweating and pushing their muscles to the limit. Their brains control their bodies and minds—they are determined to keep running and beat the other competitors.*

Did you know?

At the center of the brain stem is a message filter called the reticular formation. It acts as a watchdog for the rest of the brain. It filters all the messages coming from the spinal cord and allows only the most important ones to reach the cerebrum. This saves you having to think about unnecessary information.

Brain Power

The cerebrum consists of two large domes each covered by a folded, wrinkled layer of nerve cells called the **cortex.** The cortex contains all the thoughts and feelings that we are aware of. It allows us to reason, plan ahead, and use language. Human beings have a bigger cortex than any other animal which is why we are more intelligent. The cortex also processes and interprets information from the senses and controls the muscles. Each of the senses is controlled by a particular area of the cortex.

◀ *Playing chess involves complicated calculation and planning ahead. Both of these are controlled by the area at the front of the cortex.*

Touch and movement

The part of the cortex that deals with the sense of touch forms a band across the cortex. Messages from the touch receptors come here. The parts of the body that have a lot of touch receptors take up a larger area of the cortex. The lips and the fingers have the largest areas of all.

Next to the sensory area on the cortex is the motor area. It sends out commands to the muscles. The fingers and mouth, which use many different muscles, take up a larger area of the cortex than other parts of the body.

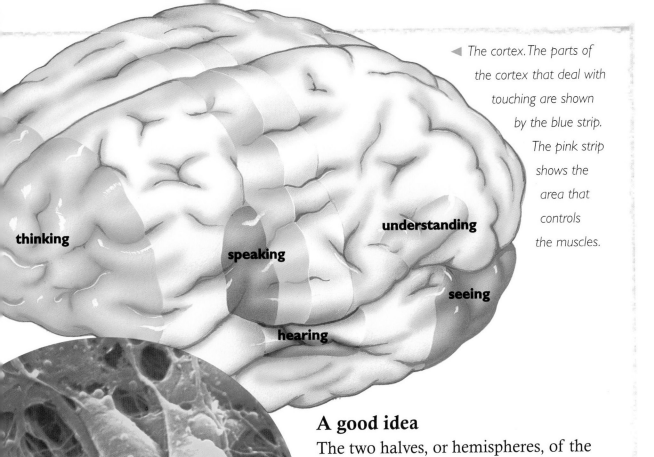

thinking

speaking

understanding

seeing

hearing

◄ The cortex. The parts of the cortex that deal with touching are shown by the blue strip. The pink strip shows the area that controls the muscles.

▲ Nerve cells in the brain look like a tangled mess, but they form pathways that allow us to learn, remember, and control our lives.

A good idea

The two halves, or hemispheres, of the cortex do not have the same jobs. The left side of the brain deals with speaking and logical thinking. The right side is more involved with creative and artistic pursuits. We all use both sides of the brain, but most people are governed more by the left side, and like to reason out a solution to a problem. People who usually jump to an answer using their intuition probably prefer to use the right side of their brain.

Did you know?

The folds on the cortex give extra room to cram in more brain cells—100 billion altogether. Each one is connected to at least 50,000 others, giving the human brain an immense capacity for learning and remembering. Unlike other cells in our body, brain cells cannot renew themselves. They die off slowly as we grow older.

27

Brain Waves

There is still much about the brain that scientists do not understand. It is difficult for them to study the brain, but they can record and study brain waves—the electrical activity of the brain. Electric wires can be lightly attached to the head. They pick up electrical signals in the brain and relay them to machines called electro-encephalographs. The machine displays the signals as an electro-encephalogram (EEG), irregular lines shown on a screen or on paper.

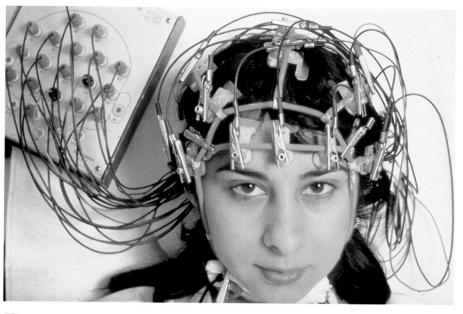

◀ An electro-encephalograph is measuring and recording the electrical signals in this girl's brain. The machine can help to detect some illnesses and to study sleep and dreams.

Dreams

You may think you do not dream very much, but scientists have discovered that most people have about five dreams a night. They know this because they have studied the EEGs of people when they are asleep. At the same time they have measured the movement of their eyes and how tense their muscles were. When you dream, the EEG changes pattern and your eyes move very fast. This is called Rapid Eye Movement or REM sleep. This type of sleep comes and goes all through the night. You are most likely to remember a dream if you are woken up in the middle of REM sleep. No one knows why we dream. Some dreams seem to be about the day's events. Other dreams may express our secret wishes and fears.

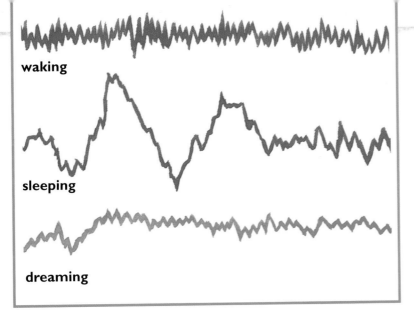

waking

sleeping

dreaming

◀ *The electro-encephalograph prints out rows of jagged lines called an electro-encephalogram (EEG). These "brain waves" form different patterns according to whether the person is alert, relaxing, thinking, sleeping dreamlessly, or dreaming.*

Brain death

At one time a person was said to have died when his or her heart stopped beating. But today machines can often restart the heart. If someone stops breathing for more than four minutes, the brain becomes starved of oxygen and brain cells begin to die. Even so, the person may still be alive. As long as the brain stem keeps working, the body stays alive, even though the person may not be aware (conscious). It is only when the brain stem fails that the person is really dead.

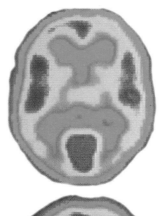
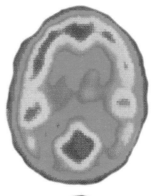
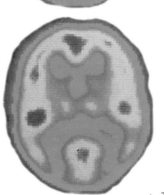
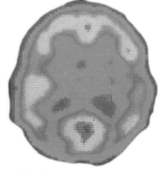

▲ *These brain scans or PET (pultron emission tomography) scans are a kind of X-ray of the brain. The red areas show which parts of the brain are working.*

Did you know?

When you are dreaming your muscles are totally relaxed. Have you ever had a nightmare when you couldn't run or scream no matter how you tried? Your muscles were too relaxed to respond! Sleepwalking and talking happen during non-dreaming sleep. The sleeper's eyes may be open, but they cannot see. And when they wake up they cannot remember anything about it.

Glossary

Acupuncture System of medicine that treats illness and pain by putting small needles into the patient's skin at particular locations.

Auditory nerves Nerves that send electrical signals to the brain, enabling us to hear.

Autonomic nervous system Part of the nervous system that controls things that happen in your bodies without you being aware of them.

Axon Long, thin extension of a nerve cell that sends electrical signals away from the cell.

Braille Writing system that uses raised dots to represent each letter of the alphabet. Blind or partially sighted people can feel the dots with their fingers and so read the words.

Brain Large mass of nerve cells that controls most of the workings of the body. The brain is situated in the head and is protected by the skull. It receives information through the senses and sensory nerves, and it controls the muscles through the motor nerves.

Brain stem Part of the brain that controls the autonomic nervous system.

Cartilage Smooth but tough gristle found that protects the ends of bones, the ear flaps and the end of the nose.

Cell The smallest unit of life. Each part of your body consists of millions of microscopic cells. Each kind of cell looks different and does a particular job. For example, nerve cells carry electrical signals, usually to or from your brain.

Cerebellum Part of the brain that lies beneath the much larger **cerebrum.** The cerebellum controls balance and coordination.

Cerebrum Largest part of the brain. It forms a dome over the rest of the brain and its nerve cells deal with sensory messages, thinking, memory, talking, and everything you are aware of.

Cochlea A part of the bony, snail-shaped passageway of the inner ear.

Cornea Transparent part of the outer eyeball that covers the iris and pupil and admits light.

Cortex Outer folded and wrinkled layer of nerve cells in the two domes that make up the **cerebrum.**

Dendrite Branched projection from a nerve cell body.

Digestive system Long tube that stretches from the mouth through the stomach and intestines to the anus. It breaks down food in the body into small particles that can be absorbed into the blood.

Electrical signals Tiny pulses of electricity. They are carried to and from the brain and within the brain by nerve cells. We experience these electrical signals as light, sound, taste, thought, memory, and feeling.

Gland Organ of the body that makes substances, such as hormones or digestive juices.

Hypothalamus Top of the brain stem. It controls body temperature and links with feelings such as thirst, hunger, anger, and pleasure.

Insulated Cut off from surroundings by a protective covering. The axons of some nerve cells are similarly insulated with fatty cells.

Light-sensitive *See* **Sensitive**.

Lungs Parts of the body that take oxygen from the air into the blood and release carbon dioxide from the blood back into the air. The lungs are in the chest. Air is breathed in and out through the nose or mouth.

Middle ear Small, membrane-lined cavity that is separated from the outer ear by the eardrums. It transmits sound waves from the eardrum to the partition between the middle and inner ears.

Motor nerves Nerves that pass messages between the brain and the muscles or glands.

Mucus Thick liquid that lines many of the inner surfaces of the body. It keeps them moist and traps germs.

Muscles Bundles of fibers that have the ability to contract (shorten) and relax. There are three types in our bodies.

Nasal passages Mucus-lined passages that lead from the nose to the throat.

Nerve Bundle of millions of nerve cells which passes electrical signals to and from and within the brain.

Nerve cells See **Cell.**

Nerve ending End of a nerve. Nerve endings detect particular kinds of stimuli by sending electrical signals along the nerves to the brain.

Nervous system Communication system that links the body and the brain. It carries information from the senses to the brain and commands from the brain to the muscles.

Optic nerve One of two nerves in the eye that carries signals to the brain.

Outer ear Part of the ear that picks up sound waves. It consists of a flap of skin and cartilage. It is the part of the year you can see.

Papilla Small raised part of the skin, for example, on the tongue or fingertip, in which a nerve ends.

Particle Small part of something. The smallest part of a substance that can exist by itself is called a molecule.

Pupil Round opening in the iris that controls the amount of light that enters the eye.

Receptors Nerve cells in the sense organs that react to a stimulus, such as light, sound or pressure, by generating an electrical signal. See also **Nerve ending.**

Reflex action Rapid action by the body as the nervous system responds to a message from sensory nerves that is relayed to motor nerves in the spinal cord.

Retina Sensory membrane that lines the eyes. It is composed of several layers. It receives the image formed by the lense and converts it into chemical and nervous signals that are sent to the brain by way of the **optic nerve.**

Sense organs Parts of the body, such as the eyes, ears, tongue, nose, and skin, that receive information from the outside world.

Senses The five senses are sight, hearing, smell, taste, and touch. When the sense organs inform the brain of changes in the environment., the brain interprets them so that we experience sight, sound, smell, and so on.

Spinal cord Bundles of nerve cells protected by the backbone. The spinal cord carries sensory and motor nerves. Messages pass along it from the senses to the brain and from the brain to the muscles.

Stimulus Something which triggers a reaction or response.

Index

acupuncture 18
anesthetics 19
autonomic nervous system 23, 25
axons 20, 21

babies 6, 9
balance, sense of 11, 25
blind people 7, 9, 17
blinking 23
Braille 7, 17
brain 4, 5, 6, 7, 8, 9, 10, 11, 12, 13, 14, 20, 21, 22, 24–9
brain scans 29
brain stem 24, 25, 29
brain waves 28–9
breathing 5, 25

cells 5, 12, 14
    brain cells 27, 29
    light-sensitive cells 8
    nerve cells 4, 5, 9, 10, 16, 20, 24, 26, 27
    skin cells 17
    taste cells 14
cerebellum 24, 25
cerebrum 24, 25, 26
coordination 7
color 8, 9
color blindness 9
cones 8, 9
cornea 8
cortex 26, 27
creativity 27

decibels 11
dendrites 20
digestive system 5, 23, 25

dreams 28, 29

ears 4, 6, 10–11, 21
electrical signals 4, 6, 8, 9, 10, 14, 20, 21, 23, 28
electro-encephalograms (EEGs) 28, 29
eyes 4, 6, 8–9, 21

fingers 16, 17, 26

"gag" reflex 15

hearing 6, 10–11
heart 21, 23, 25
hypothalamus 24, 25

intelligence 26
lips 17, 26

logical thinking 27

memory 13, 27
mouth 12, 16, 21, 26
muscles 4, 5, 7, 20, 21, 25, 26, 27, 28, 29

nasal passages 12, 13
nerve endings 8, 11, 18, 19, 20, 21
nerves 4, 6, 10, 12, 14, 20, 21
    motor nerves 20, 21, 22, 25
    optic nerve 8
    relay nerves 22
    sensory nerves 16, 20, 21, 22
nervous system 4, 22

nose 6, 12–13, 21, 23

pain 18–19, 23
papillae 14, 15
paralysis 21
pultron emission tomography (PET) scans 29
pupil of the eye 8, 23

receptors 6
    pain receptors 6, 16, 18
    smell receptors 12, 13
    touch receptors 16, 17, 26
reflex actions 22–3
reticular formation 25
retina 8, 9
rods 8, 9

sense organs 4, 5, 6, 20, 26
senses 4, 6–7, 20, 25, 26
sensitivity 16, 21
sight 6, 7, 8–9, 15
skin 5, 6, 16, 17
sleepwalking and talking 29
smell, sense of 6, 12–13,
sound waves 6, 10
speech 7, 27
spinal cord 20, 21, 22, 24, 25
stimulus 6, 14, 20
swallowing 23

tastebuds 14
taste, sense of 6, 13, 14–15
tongue 6, 14, 15, 17
touch, sense of 6, 7, 16–17, 26, 27

Further Reading

Ardley, Neil. *Science Book of the Senses*. San Diego: Gulliver/HBJ, 1992.

Asimov, Isaac. *Why Do We Need Sleep?* Milwaukee: Gareth Stevens, 1993.

Parker, Steve. *Touching a Nerve: How You Touch, Sense and Feel*. Danbury, Ct.: Franklin Watts, 1992.

Suzuki, David. *Looking At the Body*. New York: Wiley, 1991.